Spotlight on Songwriters

JACK ANTONOFF

Ursula Pang

CREATED BY Humans

Published in 2027 by The Rosen Publishing Group, Inc.
2544 Clinton Street, Buffalo, NY 14224

First Edition

Editor: Greg Roza
Designer: Michael Flynn

Photo Credits: Cover Debby Wong/Shutterstock.com; (series background) Yuliya Chsherbakova/Shutterstock.com; p. 5 Angel Marchini via ZUMA Wire/Alamy; p. 7 Daniel DeSlover/ZUMA Wire/Alamy Live News; p. 9 agwilson/Shutterstock.com; p. 11 Kathy Hutchins/Shutterstock.com; p. 13 UPI/Jim Ruymen/Alamy; p. 15 https://commons.wikimedia.org/wiki/File:Bleachers_2014.jpg; p. 17 (main) Daniel DeSlover/ZUMA Wire/Alamy Live News; p. 17 (inset) Brian Friedman/Shutterstock.com; p. 19 Adam McCullough/Shutterstock.com; p. 21 Gonzales Photo/Alamy.

Cataloging-in-Publication Data

Names: Pang, Ursula.
Title: Jack Antonoff / Ursula Pang.
Description: Buffalo, New York : Created by Humans, an imprint of Rosen Publishing, 2027. | Series: Spotlight on songwriters| Includes glossary and index.
Identifiers: ISBN 9781534553439 (pbk.) | ISBN 9781534553446 (library bound) | ISBN 9781534553453 (ebook)
Subjects: LCSH: Antonoff, Jack, 1984- --Juvenile literature. | Music producers--United States--Biography--Juvenile literature. | Musicians--United States--Biography--Juvenile literature.
Classification: LCC ML3930.A6 P36 2027 | DDC 782.42166092--dc23

Manufactured in the United States of America

CONTENTS

Talented Artist

Jack Antonoff is famous in the music world. He's a musician and singer. He's a songwriter too. He's also a producer. That means he works with other music artists to make their songs and albums even better. Jack is talented in many ways!

Young Jack

Jack was born March 31, 1984, in Bergenfield, New Jersey. He started playing guitar with his dad when he was 12. He and his friends formed a band called Outline when he was 14. They played **punk** music. They made an album and went on tour.

In 2002, Jack's younger sister Sarah died of **cancer**. Her death had a big **impact** on Jack's life and music. He said that much of his music was written while he was thinking about Sarah. Music was a way to help him deal with his sadness.

More Bands

Starting in 2001, Jack played with a new band, Steel Train. He was the lead singer. They made three albums. They played on TV shows and in **festivals**. Next, Jack was asked to join a band called fun. They made music mostly **inspired** by hip-hop and pop.

MOVIE
NEW YORK

First Grammy

Jack played many **instruments** for the band fun., including guitar, cello, piano, and drums. He also sang and wrote songs. He helped write fun.'s first hit song, "We Are Young." It won the 2013 **Grammy** for Song of the Year.

Bleachers

Jack decided to make his own music. He used the name Bleachers. He made an album in which he cowrote every song and played nearly every instrument. That album was called *Strange Desire*. The songs "I Wanna Get Better" and "Rollercoaster" were hits in 2014.

BLEACHERS

Producer

Jack is now a well-known producer too, but he wasn't always. Taylor Swift was the first artist Jack worked with as a producer. The friends have also cowritten songs, including "Out of the Woods" on Taylor's album *1989*. They worked together on other Taylor Swift albums too, including 2024's *The Tortured Poets Department*.

Taylor Swift

Jack has also produced music for the artists Lorde, Lana Del Rey, St. Vincent, Sabrina Carpenter, and Kendrick Lamar. He won the Grammy for Producer of the Year, Non-Classical in 2021, 2022, and 2023. As of 2026, he has won 13 Grammy Awards in all.

PRINCESS

Continuing to Create

Every year brings new Jack Antonoff music. In 2026, he and Taylor Swift cowrote a song called "I Knew It, I Knew You" for the movie *Toy Story 5*. He also performs each year at his music festival in New Jersey, Shadow of the City. This artist continues to make a big impact on the music world.

GLOSSARY

cancer: A disease caused by the uncontrolled growth of cells in the body.

Grammy: An award given each year in the United States to honor people who make music.

festival: A special day or days with its own social activities, food, or music.

impact: A powerful effect.

inspire: To give someone an idea of what to create.

instrument: An object used to make music.

punk: A kind of fast, loud music that was first popular among young people in the late 1970s.

FOR MORE INFORMATION

BOOKS

Monteagudo, Susana. *Illustrated History of Rock*. Berkeley, CA: Gingko Press, 2023.

Nelson, Kristen Rajczak. *Taylor Swift's Songwriting: Love, Poetry, and Addressing the Haters.* Buffalo, NY: Gareth Stevens Publishing, 2025.

WEBSITES

Artist: Jack Antonoff
grammy.com/artists/jack-antonoff/248/
Read about the Grammy Awards Jack has won so far.

Jack Antonoff
www.britannica.com/biography/Jack-Antonoff
Britannica offers more facts about this talented artist.

INDEX